| | DATE DUE | | |
|---|---|---|---|

Donated $30.35

J612.8

Parker,Steve

Body Focus     SPINAL CORD AND
NERVES

Injury,Illness and Health

J612.8

Parker,Steve

Body Focus     SPINAL CORD AND NERVES

Injury,Illness and Health

# Spinal Cord and Nerves

## Injury, Illness and Health

**Steve Parker**

Heinemann Library
Chicago, Illinois

Customer Service  888-454-2279

Visit our website at www.heinemannlibrary.com

Design: Jo Hinton-Malivoire and AMR
Illustrations: Art Construction

Originated by Blenheim Colour Ltd
Printed in China by Wing King Tong

07 06 05 04 03
10 9 8 7 6 5 4 3 2 1

**Library of Congress Cataloging-in-Publication Data**
Parker, Steve.
    Spinal cord and nerves / Steve Parker.
        p. cm. -- (Body focus)
    Includes bibliographical references and index.
    Contents: The nervous system -- The spinal cord -- Around the spinal cord -- Inside the spinal cord -- Peripheral nerves -- Inside a nerve -- Nerve cells -- How nerve signals work.
    ISBN 1-4034-0753-3 (HC), 1-4034-3301-1 (Pbk.)
    1. Nervous system--Juvenile literature. 2. Nerves--Juvenile literature. 3. Spinal cord--Juvenile literature. [1. Nervous system. 2. Nerves. 3. Spinal cord.] I. Title. II. Series.
    QP361.5.P374 2003
    612.8--dc21

                    2002152970

**Acknowledgments**
The author and publisher are grateful to the following for permission to reproduce copyright material: pp. 5, 13, 29 Getty Images; p. 11 Sporting Pictures; p. 15 SPL/GJP-CNRI; p. 16 SPL/Deep Light Productions; p. 19 SPL/David Gifford; pp. 21, 37 Actionplus; p. 25 SPL/Will & Deni McIntyre; p. 28 Kit Houghton/Houghton's Horses; p. 30 SPL/Mauro Fermariello; pp. 31, 43 SPL; p. 33 AP/Eric Draper; p. 34 SPL/John Radcliffe Hospital; p. 35 Imaging Body; p. 38 SPL/Dr John Zajicek; p. 39 Corbis/Bryn Colton/Assignments; p. 40 SPL/BSIP, Laurent/Pioffet; p. 42 SPL/James King-Holmes.

The computer tomography scan of the lower spine on the cover is produced courtesy of Science Photo Library/GJLP.

The publisher would like to thank David Wright and Kelley Staley for their assistance with the preparation of this book.

Some words are shown in bold, **like this.** You can find out what they mean by looking in the glossary.

# CONTENTS

# THE NERVOUS SYSTEM

The human body contains hundreds of different parts, such as the stomach, intestines, liver, kidneys, brain, bones, muscles, and heart. Each has its own tasks to do. However, all the parts must work together, in a controlled and coordinated way, so that the body can function as a whole and stay healthy.

## Controlling the body

Two systems in the body control all of its parts, ensuring that they work together. They are the nervous system and the hormonal system. The nervous system has three main parts—the brain, the spinal cord, and the nerves. This book focuses on the latter parts of the nervous system: the spinal cord and the nerves.

## Two similar systems

In some ways, the body's nervous system is similar to the communications systems you use daily to make phone calls, send e-mails, and surf the Internet. The nervous system as well as communciations systems are designed in the form of a network, with millions of senders, receivers, and connections. These systems work to send information or messages from one place to another. Messages travel in the form of tiny electrical signals or pulses, along bundles of long, wirelike structures. In these systems, there are parts called relay stations, which pass messages on to their destination.

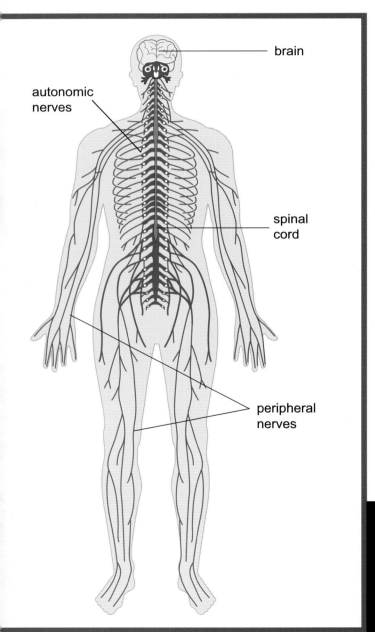

brain

autonomic nerves

spinal cord

peripheral nerves

The nervous system has three main parts: the brain in the head, the spinal cord extending down the back, and the peripheral nerves throughout the body.

The human body's nervous system is made up of three systems that work together, as described below.

## Central nervous system

The central nervous system consists of the brain and spinal cord. The brain is the most important part, because it is the site of thoughts, feelings, emotions, desires, ideas, and memories. The spinal cord links the brain to many parts of the body.

## Peripheral nervous system

The **peripheral** nervous system is the network of nerves that branch from the brain and spinal cord to every body part. It carries messages around the body, to and from the brain and spinal cord. Some of these messages are about sensations, such as what the eyes see or what the skin touches. Other messages are about **voluntary** body movements.

## Autonomic nervous system

The third part of the nervous system is the **autonomic** nervous system. This system deals with autonomic, or automatic, body processes. These processes are **involuntary** and include the heartbeat, digestion, and removal of wastes.

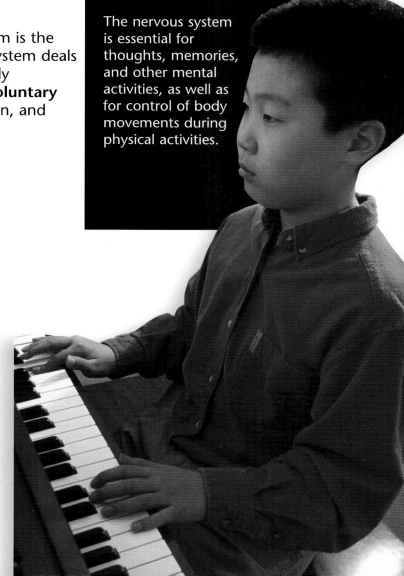

The nervous system is essential for thoughts, memories, and other mental activities, as well as for control of body movements during physical activities.

### Neurology
The medical study of the brain, spinal cord, and nerves; how they work; and the disorders that affect them is known as neurology. A neurologist is a doctor who specializes in problems of the nervous system. A neurosurgeon performs operations on these body parts.

# NERVE CELLS

The nervous system is made up of more than 100 billion nerve **cells** called neurons. Most are in the brain and spinal cord. Compared to other types of cells, they live for a very long time. Skin cells, for example, live only about one month, and blood cells live three months. However, nerve cells last many years.

## Features of a nerve cell

A typical nerve cell has three main parts: a **cell body, dendrites,** and an **axon.**

The cell body of a nerve cell is much the same as that of other cells. It has a control center, or **nucleus,** and other cell parts. In most nerve cells, the cell body is about one-thousandth of an inch (.025 millimeter) wide.

## Dendrites

Dendrites are long, thin branches that grow from the cell body. They extend outward like a spider web, branching and becoming thinner. They are so long that their ends almost touch other nerve cells. The main task of the dendrites is to receive nerve messages from other nerve cells and carry them toward the cell body.

## Axons

The axon, also called the nerve fiber, is a long, thick, wirelike branch of the cell body. It may have its own fingerlike branches at its end. The main task of the axon is to carry nerve messages away from the cell body and pass them to other nerve cells.

A nerve cell, or neuron, has a cell body similar to other cells, long extensions called dendrites, and an even longer axon.

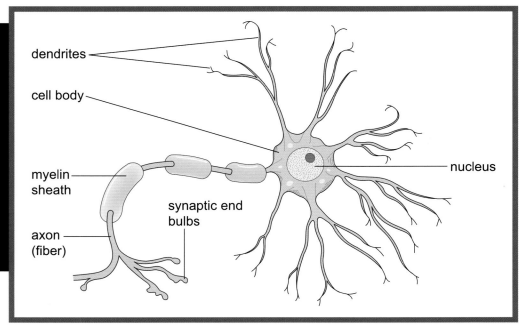

Nerve cells have many designs. Some have very short axons, or several axons. Some have just a few dendrites, while others have thousands. Some nerve cells have a cell body located halfway along the axon, while others have a cell body located near one end.

## Types of axons

There are two main kinds of axons: **myelinated** and unmyelinated.

A myelinated axon has a covering, or sheath, wrapped around it. The sheath is made of a special kind of cell called the Schwann cell. As the Schwann cell grows, it wraps itself around the axon several times, like rolling a sheet of plastic around a long pole. The outer layer, or **membrane,** of the Schwann cell makes a fatty substance called myelin.

The myelin sheath works like the plastic coating on an electric wire. It keeps a nerve signal from leaking or becoming weaker as it passes along the axon. It also helps the nerve signal travel faster along the axon—about 328 feet (100 meters) per second or even more.

One myelin sheath does not usually stretch the whole length of the axon. There are several sheaths, one after another, separated by tiny gaps called nodes. A nerve signal travels fastest between nodes, jumping from one to the next.

An unmyelinated axon has no covering of myelin. It carries nerve messages more slowly, usually about 3.3 to 6.6 feet (1 to 2 meters) per second.

Most axons in the spinal cord and **peripheral** nerves are myelinated. In the brain, many are unmyelinated.

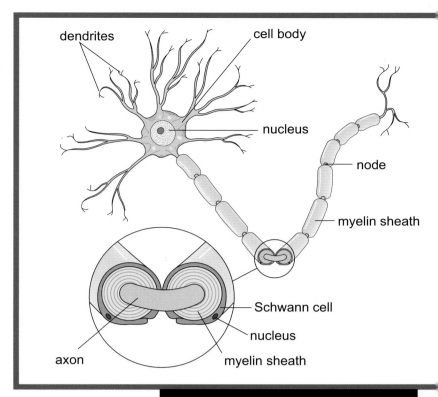

A myelinated axon has a series of coverings called myelin sheaths wrapped around it. Each sheath is a single cell called a Schwann cell. It grows in a spiral fashion around the axon and contains the fatty substance called myelin. The dendrites do not have coverings.

### The longest cells

Some nerve cell axons in the nerves of the arms and legs are more than 23.6 inches (60 centimeters) in length. These nerve cells are by far the longest cells in the body. Despite their length, each single axon is far too thin to see with the unaided eye.

# INSIDE A NERVE

A typical nerve looks pale gray or white and is smooth and shiny. The thickest **peripheral** nerve is the sciatic nerve, which is found in the hip and upper leg. It is nearly as wide as a thumb. The thinnest peripheral nerves are as narrow as hairs. Thick or thin, most nerves have the same basic structure.

## Outer covering

A nerve has a tough, **fibrous** outer covering, or sheath. This protects it from being twisted, kinked, or squashed. Inside the nerve are long **axons.** Each axon comes from a single nerve **cell.** A thick main nerve has hundreds of thousands of axons. Very small and thin nerves, such as those that control the small muscles that move the eyeball, have just a few dozen axons.

## Bundles of axons

The axons are grouped into bundles called fascicles. Usually, the axons in one bundle are all **sensory** or all **motor axons.** Some nerves contain only bundles of motor axons and are called motor nerves. Others contain only sensory axons and are known as sensory nerves. However, many nerves are mixed, with some bundles of sensory axons and some bundles of motor axons.

In addition to axons, most nerves also contain tiny **blood vessels** that supply nourishment and take away waste. They also have a fatty substance that provides cushioning between and around the bundles.

## Ganglia

Along many nerves are lumplike bulges known as **ganglia.** Ganglia are collections of nerve cell bodies whose axons pass along the length of the nerve. The nerve cell bodies are surrounded by satellite cells, which supply nourishment and take away waste. Ganglia also contain supporting axons and tiny blood vessels.

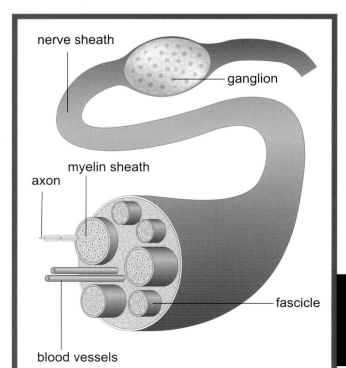

nerve sheath

ganglion

myelin sheath

axon

fascicle

blood vessels

A typical nerve contains several bundles of long nerve axons, wrapped in tough coverings known as fascicles.

## Gone to sleep

Sometimes you sit or lie in an awkward position, with one part of the body pressing on another, or with a joint bent in an unusual way. This can squash a nerve or its blood supply, which prevents the nerve from working normally. Numbness or loss of feeling, and perhaps aching, warn of the problem. The part may not be able to move. When this occurs, it is said that the body part has gone to sleep.

## Pins and needles

After a body part has gone to sleep, you stretch or move it to relieve the problem. The nerve and its blood supply begin to work again, giving a tingling, or pins and needles, sensation as the nerve signals start to pass along it. Rubbing the part and flexing its joints also help to speed recovery.

## Naming nerves

Individual nerves are usually named after the part of the body through which they pass, or from the name of a nearby muscle or bone. For example, the ulnar nerve runs down the inner side of the arm. It is named after the ulna, the bone in the lower arm along which it lies.

Each branch of each main nerve also has its own name. As a result, there are hundreds of medical names for nerves, one for each of the body's peripheral nerves.

In most human bodies, the main nerves follow a similar branching pattern into the major body parts and organs. However, there is variation among individual people, in the length and branching of the smaller nerves.

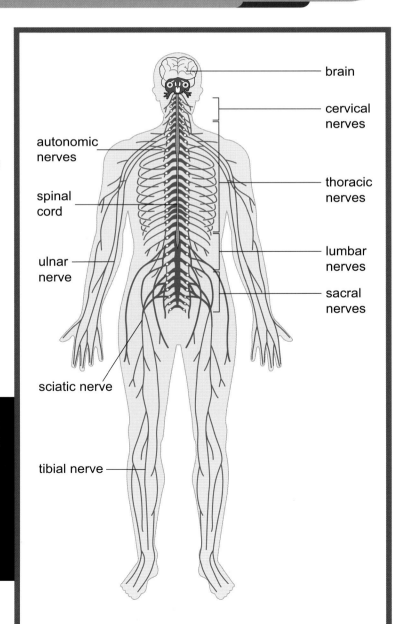

brain

cervical nerves

autonomic nerves

thoracic nerves

spinal cord

ulnar nerve

lumbar nerves

sacral nerves

sciatic nerve

tibial nerve

# HOW NERVE SIGNALS WORK

Every second, millions of nerve signals pass through the body's nervous system, especially up and down the spinal cord, and around the brain. A single nerve signal is a tiny, brief pulse of electricity. It has the strength of about 0.1 volts (a standard flashlight battery is 1.5 volts). It lasts only about one millisecond—that is, one-thousandth of a second.

## At the membrane

A nerve signal does not pass along the inside of a nerve **cell**. It passes along its outer layer, or cell **membrane**. The signal is made by the movement of substances called **ions**. These are natural body chemicals, dissolved and floating in the watery liquid on both sides of the cell membrane. Because ions are dissolved, they have charges. They are either positive or negative. The main ions are sodium and potassium. Both have positive charges.

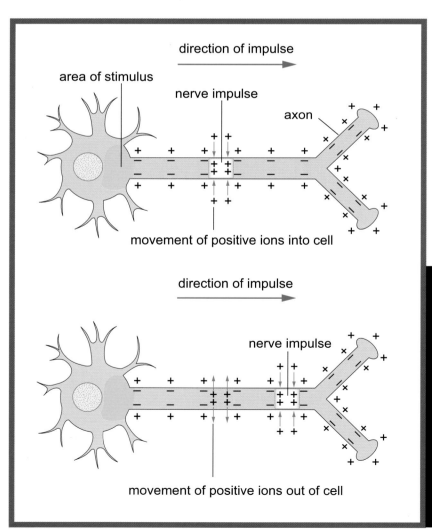

direction of impulse

area of stimulus

nerve impulse

axon

movement of positive ions into cell

direction of impulse

nerve impulse

movement of positive ions out of cell

The nerve cell's membrane has tiny structures in it called ion pumps. These pass, or push, certain ions through the membrane, which normally acts as a barrier. The movements of the charged ions across the cell membrane make a nerve signal, as shown in the diagram here.

A nerve signal, or impulse, is a tiny burst of electricity formed by the movements of dissolved substances called ions. These pass into and out of the nerve cell, across its outer covering, or membrane. The main ions are sodium and potassium, which have a positive charge. This process is chemical rather than physical, but it still uses energy.

## The nerve pulse

When there is no nerve signal, there are more sodium ions outside the cell membrane, in the fluid around the nerve cell, than there are inside the membrane. Conversely, there are more potassium ions inside the nerve cell than outside.

As a nerve signal arrives at a region of cell membrane, sodium pumps push sodium ions into the nerve cell. Then, potassium pumps push potassium ions outside the cell. These rapid movements of positive ions cause a spike of electricity, known as the action potential, which is the nerve signal.

The next region of membrane does the same, and the next, and so on. This causes the message to travel along the cell's membrane as a wave of moving ions, which creates a flowing electrical pulse.

As people stand and lift their arms, then sit, a wave passes along a crowd. In a similar way, ions move in and out of a nerve cell to form the moving wave of a nerve signal.

## A moving wave

The movement of sodium ions across the membrane of a nerve cell is called depolarization. The traveling nerve signal is called a wave of depolarization. After it passes, the ions move more slowly, back to their normal positions. During this time, called the refractory period, no signal can pass through the cell.

Most nerve cells carry a few nerve signals each second, even when they have no information to send. As they send more information, they carry more signals closer together, up to 300 per second.

### The size of a nerve cell
The **dendrites** and **axons** of a nerve cell can be very long. If a nerve cell body was enlarged to the size of a soccer ball, the branching web of dendrites could be big enough to fill a house. The axon might be much longer—more than half a mile (1 kilometer) in length.

Nerve **cells** carry nerve messages as tiny electrical signals and pass them to other nerve cells. However, nerve cells do not actually touch each other. They are separated by tiny gaps called **synapses.** Nerve messages pass, or jump, across the gaps not as waves of electricity but as body chemicals.

## A gap in the way

At the nerve junction, or synapse, the cell **membranes** of two nerve cells are separated by a tiny gap, about one-hundredth of the width of a human hair. This gap is wide enough to prevent the passage of the wave of electricity of a nerve message.

When the electrical pulse reaches the synapse, it causes the release of chemicals known as **neurotransmitters.** These flow across the gap from the sending nerve cell and touch the membrane of the receiving nerve cell. The chemicals fit into special landing sites called **receptors.** This alters the receiving membrane in such a way that the original wave of electricity begins again. The whole process is very quick; it only takes about one-thousandth of a second.

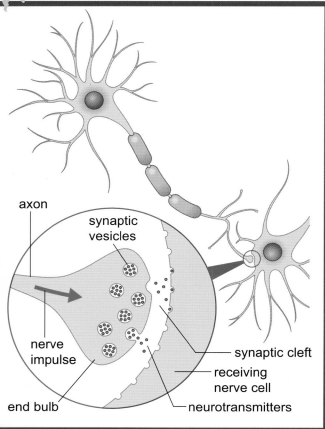

axon

synaptic vesicles

nerve impulse

end bulb

synaptic cleft

receiving nerve cell

neurotransmitters

The circle in this diagram shows an enlarged view of the synapse between two nerve cells. A tiny gap, the synaptic cleft, separates the cells.

## Go and stop

Sometimes a receiving nerve cell fires its own nerve signal after it receives just one pulse from a sending nerve cell. In other cases, it only fires its own signal after receiving several nerve pulses in quick succession, either from one sending nerve cell or from several. This effect is called summation.

Instead of telling the receiving nerve cell to fire, some nerve signals actually prevent it from firing. These are known as inhibitory signals, rather than excitatory signals.

In addition, a nerve cell does not simply pass on its messages to one other nerve cell. Most nerve cells have hundreds, even thousands, of synapses, with hundreds or thousands of other nerve cells. So the possible pathways for nerve messages between nerve cells are almost endless.

In a relay race, the baton is passed from one runner to the next. Nerve cells also pass on, or relay, their messages from one to another.

## Types of neurotransmitters

So far, medical scientists have discovered more than 50 body chemicals that work as neurotransmitters. The real number could be far higher. Several neurotransmitters in the spinal cord and **peripheral** nerve types are shown in the chart below. They are important because some medical drugs copy or block their effects and so help treat problems with the nervous system.

*Acetylcholine:*
- main neurotransmitter for the peripheral nervous system
- present where a nerve joins a muscle, at the neuromuscular junction (**motor** end plate)
- drugs that block acetylcholine are used to reduce unwanted muscle action and to widen the pupils during eye examination.

*Glycine:*
- has mainly an inhibitory effect, reducing nerve signals that are less important in the spinal cord
- allows important nerve signals to be sent to and from the brain.

*Norepinephrine:*
- occurs in the nervous system, controlling internal processes, such as production of body heat, and also acts as a **hormone**
- involved in the body's general level of arousal or awareness
- also involved in the nerves of the **autonomic,** or automatic, nervous system.

*Endorphins:*
- occur especially in the spinal cord
- reduce, or inhibit, nerve cells that carry nerve signals for pain
- some painkilling medical drugs are based on endorphins, blocking pain signals passing up the spinal cord.

# SPINAL CORD AND SPINAL COLUMN

The spinal cord is the main link between the brain and the body. It could be described as a long, thin extension of the brain itself. It is the largest single nerve in the body. The spinal cord is located inside a tunnel, called the vertebral tunnel, within the backbone, or spinal column. The tunnel is made up of a row of holes. Each hole goes through one of the vertebral bones, or vertebrae, of the spinal column.

In an average-sized adult, the spinal cord is about 17.7 inches (45 centimeters) long and about .40 inch (1 centimeter) in diameter. This is about the width of your little finger.

## The body's main nerve

Along its length, the spinal cord joins with 31 pairs of spinal nerves (see page 22). These branch outward from the spinal cord into the body, carrying nerve messages back and forth between the spinal cord and hundreds of body parts.

At its upper end, the spinal cord merges with the base of the brain. At its lower end, it tapers to a pointed end at about the level of the navel. It does not run down to the base of the spinal column. Spinal nerves from the lower portion of the cord then run down through the rest of the vertebral tunnel to the base of the spinal column. They branch outward to the lower body, hips, and legs.

## Joints in the backbone

Each pair of spinal nerves joins the spinal cord at a small gap between two of the vertebrae that make up the backbone. The gap is formed where the bones are linked at a joint. Between the two bones, there is a cushion-like pad of tough but slightly flexible **cartilage** known as the intervertebral disk. It holds the two vertebrae slightly apart, creating the gap for spinal nerves to join the spinal cord.

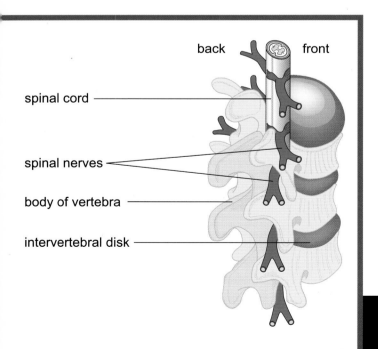

back    front

spinal cord

spinal nerves

body of vertebra

intervertebral disk

The spinal cord is inside the spinal column, in a row of holes through the vertebrae.

In this side view of the backbone, a disk between two vertebrae (individual spine bones) has become misshapen and presses on the spinal cord, causing pain and partial paralysis.

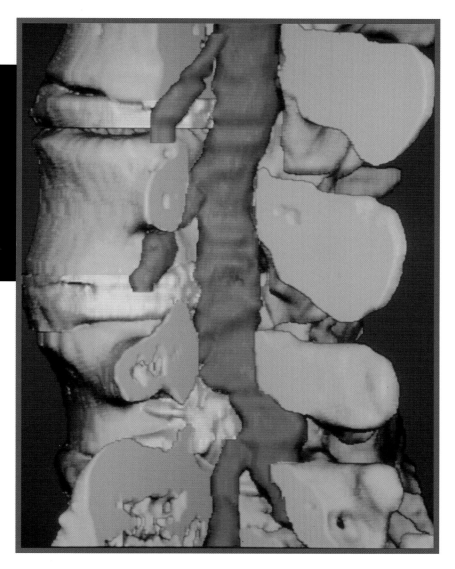

## Disks in the backbone

The intervertebral disk allows the two vertebral bones to tilt, or twist, slightly. Over the whole length of the backbone, the small movements at each of these joints work together so that the neck and back can twist and bend.

The spinal cord is well protected within the spinal column, safe from knocks, twists, kinks and pressure. However, sometimes a disk can press on a spinal nerve and cause problems.

## Prolapsed, or slipped, disk

The intervertebral disk between two vertebral bones may be weak for some reason, such as from a back injury. Or it can become excessively squeezed, for example, when a person suddenly carries very heavy weights. The disk may bulge, or prolapse, at a weak point. The bulge may press on a spinal nerve, or on the spinal cord itself. This can cause pain and perhaps numbness or weakness of the parts supplied by that nerve. The problem is sometimes called a slipped disk, but this name is misleading. It is very rare for the whole disk to slip out of position. Usually, the problem is due to the bulge, or prolapse.

# PROTECTING THE SPINAL CORD AND NERVES

When some parts of the body are injured or diseased, they can repair themselves. For example, a scrape on the skin soon heals as new skin forms. Nerve **cells**, however, have very complicated shapes and millions of delicate connections. They are so specialized that they cannot normally multiply to replace themselves, as part of everyday body maintenance. As a result, the natural process of repair to the nervous system is very slow and, in some cases, may not be possible at all.

## Long-term outlook

The long-term nature of nerve damage makes it is vitally important to avoid injury or harm, especially to the brain, spinal cord, and nerves. Injury can occur just as easily during a short car trip as it can while engaging in extreme sports such as snowboarding and skydiving. If measures are not take to avoid injury, the result can be a broken neck or back, with far-reaching effects on daily life.

## Care and precautions

The best way to avoid injury is to use protective clothing and equipment. This includes helmets, visors and head guards, neck and back braces, shoulder and hip pads, elbow and knee guards, wrist guards, gloves, shin guards, and ankle and foot protectors.

This equipment is designed to prevent all kinds of injury, from wounds, sprained joints and broken bones to trapped or crushed nerves and a broken neck or back. Some cases of nerve damage occur when a body part is pulled or wrenched violently, and a bone or joint crushes a nearby nerve.

Serious back injury can be caused by a fall from a cliff—or even from a chair.

Carpal tunnel syndrome affects a nerve in the wrist called the median nerve. This nerve runs through a tunnel formed by the bones of the wrist and the carpal ligament, which wraps around the inside of the wrist similar to a watch band.

The median nerve may be squeezed, or compressed, due to a wrist injury or to a disorder that affects the joint, such as arthritis. Another cause is tendinitis. The long tendons of the forearm muscles pass through the wrist to move the fingers. These tendons may become sore, swollen, and painful to people who use their fingers every day in repeated actions, such as typing on a computer keyboard.

Compression of the median nerve produces tingling and numbness in parts of the hand. It may cause pain that becomes worse at night. It can also make delicate finger movements difficult. Treatment varies from rest or injections of **anti-inflammatory** medications to surgery to loosen the carpal ligament.

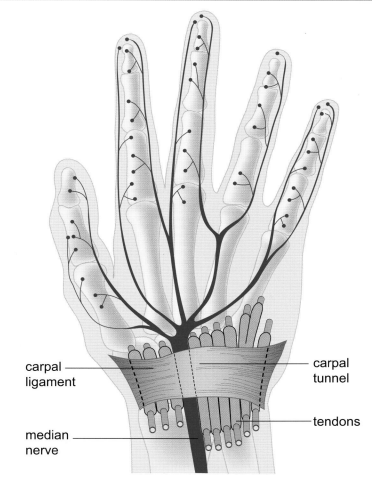

carpal ligament

carpal tunnel

median nerve

tendons

The main nerve in the wrist passes through a gap or tunnel, under the bandlike carpal ligament and between muscle tendons to the hand. In carpal tunnel syndrome, the nerve is put under pressure and becomes inflamed.

## Training and coaching
For almost any sort of activity, the right kind of training routine can help to prevent injury. Training strengthens muscles and joints, and it teaches movement control. This makes accidents, sprains, strains, and nerve damage less likely. A coach or supervisor can also explain the dangers and hazards of an activity. He or she can advise on how to get out of a dangerous situation with the least harm. For example, he or she can teach a person how to fall in a way that avoids injury.

# AROUND THE SPINAL CORD

The spinal cord is narrower than the tunnel through which it runs within the bones of the spinal column. Filling the space between the outside of the cord and the inside of the bony tunnel are three sheetlike layers called **meninges.** They wrap around the spinal cord like three long bags, one inside the other. At the upper end of the spinal cord, where it merges with the brain, the meninges continue and wrap around the brain itself.

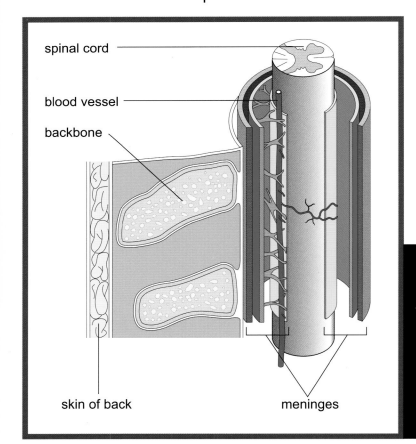

spinal cord

blood vessel

backbone

skin of back

meninges

The three layers of the meninges form a cushion around the spinal cord. It's similar to wrapping a valuable item in foam rubber or bubble wrap. The meninges protect the cord from sudden knocks, kinks, twists, and jars inside its tunnel within the backbone.

The meninges wrap around the spinal cord. The outer layer nearest the backbone is the dura mater. The middle layer, with extensive blood vessels, is the arachnoid. There is a fluid-filled gap between it and the inner layer, the pia mater, which covers the cord itself.

## Fluid around the cord

There is a slight gap between the middle and the innermost of the three meninges layers. This is not an empty space, however. It contains a special liquid known as cerebrospinal fluid (CSF). This fluid also fills the central canal, which is the tiny hole along the middle of the spinal cord.

The meninges extend above the spinal cord and around the brain. The CSF also extends around the brain. In fact, it is made inside the brain, at the rate of a few teaspoonfuls each day. The fluid oozes in a slow, one-way flow around the brain and down around the spinal cord. It seeps slowly out through the meninges, at the same rate it is made, and into the general **blood vessels** nearby.

## What does CSF do?

CSF contains substances that nourish the spinal cord, including oxygen and various **minerals**. It also contains germ-fighting white blood **cells,** and it collects waste substances from around the spinal cord, which it carries away into the blood.

In addition, CSF helps the meninges protect the spinal cord. It forms a water-cushion around the spinal cord to protect it from sudden knocks and jarring.

## Importance of CSF

Unusual substances in CSF can suggest certain health problems:

- Increased **gamma globulin** in CSF may indicate multiple sclerosis.
- The presence of blood in CSF may indicate bleeding, or a **hemorrhage,** around the brain or spinal cord.
- Certain germs in CSF can confirm an infection, such as meningitis.

A small sample of CSF may be taken for tests, in a procedure called lumbar puncture.

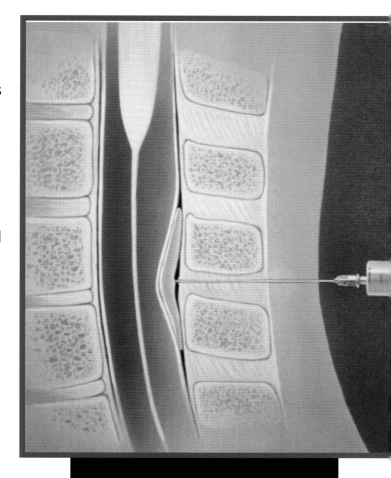

This illustration shows an epidural taking place. A needle is inserted between two vertebrae to inject an anesthetic.

## Lumbar puncture

A small sample of CSF is usually taken by lumbar puncture, or spinal tap. A hollow needle is inserted, with great care, through the skin and muscles of the lower back (the lumbar spine), between two vertebrae, and into the meninges. A sample of CSF is withdrawn into a syringe for tests. A similar procedure, known as epidural anesthetic, is used to inject drugs that relieve pain during childbirth or during an operation on the lower body.

# INSIDE THE SPINAL CORD

From the outside, the spinal cord looks like a pale gray cord with pairs of similar-colored nerves branching from it. Inside, an H-shaped darker center is surrounded by a much paler area. These two areas are known as gray and white matter, and under a microscope they look very different from each other.

## Gray and white matter

The H-shaped area of gray matter is actually pinkish-gray. It contains the main parts, or **cell bodies,** of nerve **cells,** along with their short, spiderlike connections known as **dendrites.** There are very few **axons.**

In the gray matter, nerve messages are passed between nerve cells. They are routed back and forth as they arrive from the brain above and travel to body parts along the spinal nerves, or as they come in from body parts to be sent to the brain.

White matter contains mainly long, wirelike axons. They serve as nerve highways, carrying the tiny electrical pulses that make up nerve messages.

Compared to a telephone system, the white matter is similar to the bundles of electrical cables or optical fibers that carry messages at high speeds over long distances. The gray matter is similar to a mixture of telephones, computers, and exchanges, where the messages are sent and received, sorted, and processed.

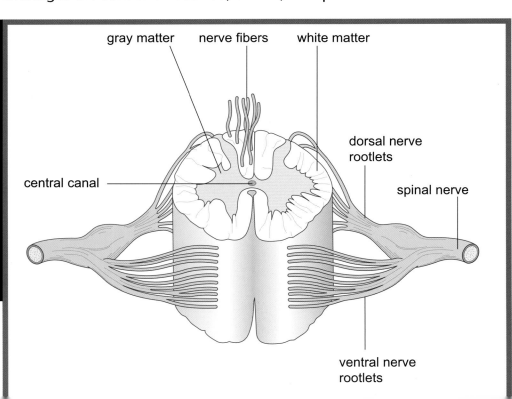

This cut-through view of the spinal cord shows a central area of gray matter surrounded by white matter of axons.

gray matter    nerve fibers    white matter

dorsal nerve rootlets

central canal

spinal nerve

ventral nerve rootlets

## Sensory signals

All nerve messages are made up of tiny electrical signals. There are two kinds of nerve messages, depending on where they are going.

**Sensory** messages come from the body's sense organs and other parts and travel to the brain. The sensory parts include the eyes, ears, nose, tongue, and skin. There are also sensors inside the body that detect temperature, blood pressure, and other conditions.

## Motor signals

**Motor** messages travel in the opposite way—from the brain, out into the body. Most are sent to muscles, telling them when to pull and by how much so that the body can move. Other motor messages control the heart, intestines, and other internal parts. Also, some motor messages travel to body parts called **glands.** These motor messages control the release of contents from the gland, such as saliva from the salivary glands in the face.

### White matter and nerve tracts

In the spinal cord's white matter, the axons are found in bundles, or groups, called tracts. There are two kinds of tracts:

- Ascending tracts carry sensory messages that come from spinal nerves, up the spinal cord, and to the brain.
- Descending tracts convey motor messages from the brain, down the spinal cord, and then out along spinal nerves to muscles and glands.

In fast sports, such as table tennis, nerve signals flash up and down the spinal cord, between the brain and the body, at the rate of millions every second.

# PERIPHERAL NERVES

There are 31 pairs of spinal nerves that branch from each side of the spinal cord. These nerves snake out through the body, dividing into smaller and smaller branches. They reach into every part of the body, from the top of the head to the tips of the fingers and toes.

This huge and complicated network of nerves is called the **peripheral** nervous system. It is estimated that if all the peripheral nerves from one body were joined end to end, they would circle the earth three times!

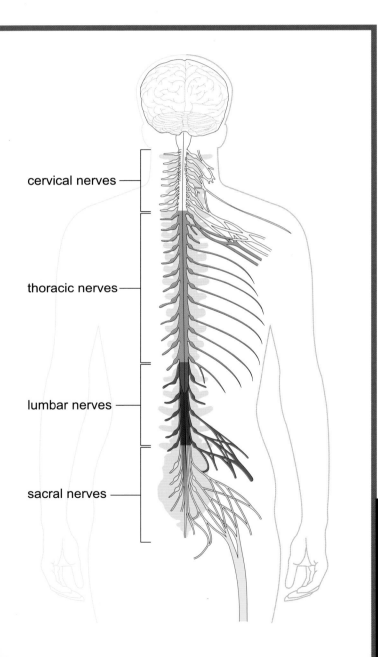

cervical nerves

thoracic nerves

lumbar nerves

sacral nerves

## Where the nerves go

There are four main groups of spinal nerve pairs. The eight pairs of cervical spinal nerves come out from the upper part of the spinal cord. They go to the neck, shoulders, and outside part of the arms. Twelve pairs of thoracic spinal nerves curve around the front and back of the chest, between the ribs, and along the inside part of the arms. Five pairs of lumbar spinal nerves branch out into the small of the back, the hips, and the front and side of each leg. Five pairs of sacral spinal nerves lead to the groin, buttocks, and the back of each leg and ankle. The single pair of coccygeal spinal nerves, at the base of the spinal cord, go to a small part of the groin and buttock area.

The main groups of spinal nerves are named after the body parts they branch into, such as the thoracic nerves, which spread into the thorax, or chest. The sacral nerves branch out from the sacrum, which is the rear part of the hip bone, or pelvis.

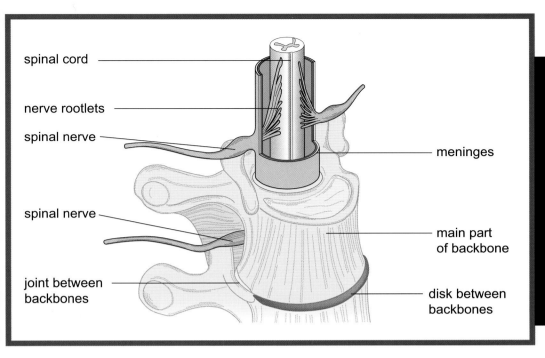

spinal cord

nerve rootlets

spinal nerve

meninges

spinal nerve

main part
of backbone

joint between
backbones

disk between
backbones

The part of a spinal nerve near the spinal cord is called a rootlet. Rootlets split into even smaller rootlets that are connected to the cord.

## Nerve roots

Near the spinal cord, each spinal nerve divides into two parts called nerve roots. The dorsal nerve root arches around to the rear of the spinal cord, while the ventral nerve root curves around to the front.

Within about .40 inch (1 centimeter) of the spinal cord, each spinal nerve root divides into many smaller rootlets, like the fingers of a tiny hand. It is these rootlets that merge into the spinal cord.

The two roots of each spinal nerve carry different messages. The dorsal nerve root carries **sensory** nerve signals into the spinal cord, mainly from the skin. The ventral nerve root carries **motor** nerve signals from the spinal cord to the muscles and **glands.**

## Cranial nerves

The peripheral nervous system also includes twelve pairs of cranial nerves. These branch out from the brain itself, rather than from the spinal cord. They connect the brain directly to the main sense organs in the head—the eyes, ears, nose, mouth, and skin. They also link the brain directly to muscles in the face, head, and neck, including the muscles for speaking and swallowing. One cranial nerve, called the vagus, has branches that pass down through the neck to parts in the midsection of the body, such as the heart and stomach.

# NERVE REFLEXES

The brain does not control the body's every movement. The spinal cord and **peripheral** nerves can work on their own. They receive nerve signals from the body's **sensory** organs and then send signals to the muscles to tell them to move. These actions usually take place automatically, without the involvement of the brain. However, the brain may become aware of them a second or two later. Such rapid, automatic reactions are called **reflexes.**

## Withdrawal reflex

There are more than twenty reflex actions. In the withdrawal reflex, pain or an unusual sensation in the fingers or hand causes the arm to suddenly pull away. For example, if the fingers touch something hot, the hand is quickly jerked away. The same happens in the leg, if the toes or foot senses pain.

These reflex reactions help protect the body from harm or injury. Even if the brain is busy thinking about something else, such as what the eyes see, the body still reacts in a split second, and the reflex helps reduce possible damage.

## Stretch reflexes

Several reflexes help us to stand and walk almost without thinking. Usually, you are not aware of these reflexes unless one of them is tested on its own. An example is the knee-jerk reflex. To test this reflex, a person sits up, crosses one knee over the other, and then another person taps the upper knee just below the kneecap. This action stretches the tendon under the skin. In the reflex response, the thigh muscles straighten the knee, causing the foot to kick out. This reflex occurs naturally if the knee suddenly bends or sags when the body is supposed to be standing upright. The reflex response straightens the knee to support the body firmly again.

In the knee-jerk reflex, a sensory nerve cell sends messages directly to a motor nerve cell.

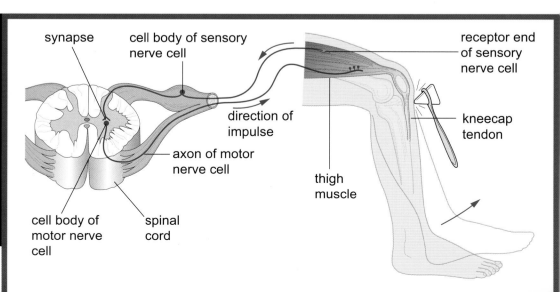

synapse

cell body of sensory nerve cell

receptor end of sensory nerve cell

direction of impulse

kneecap tendon

axon of motor nerve cell

thigh muscle

cell body of motor nerve cell

spinal cord

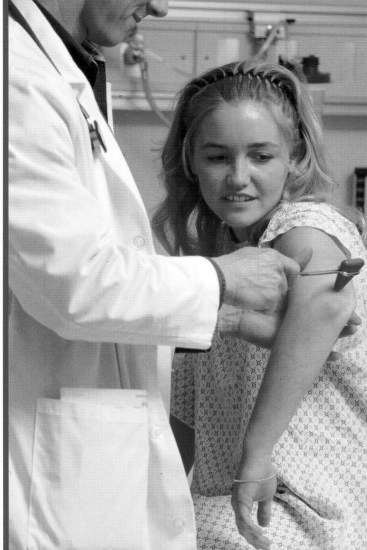

## Testing reflexes

Doctors test reflexes to obtain valuable information about nerve system damage or other problems. For example, if the knee-jerk reflex does not work properly, this may suggest damage to the spinal cord in the lower back. A similar reflex occurs at the elbow. If this reflex does not work properly, there may be spinal cord or nerve damage in the neck area.

The elbow-jerk reflex is one that can be easily tested. The body has many other reflexes, too—in the hands and feet, limbs and back, and even the eyes.

## Reflex pathways

A typical reflex involves two or three sets of nerve **cells.** The first set is made up of sensory nerve cells. They detect a change, for example, a painful sensation in the skin, and send signals along their peripheral nerve, into the spinal cord.

Inside the spinal cord, there may be a second set of nerve cells, called interneurons. These receive incoming sensory messages and pass them on to **motor** nerve cells. In most cases, interneurons also send messages up the spinal cord to the brain. This makes us aware that the reflex is happening, although you cannot stop or control it.

The third set is made up of motor nerve cells. They convey nerve signals from the spinal cord and out to the muscles that carry out the movement. If there are no interneurons, signals pass directly from the sensory nerve cells to the motor nerve cells inside the spinal cord.

# AUTONOMIC NERVOUS SYSTEM

If you had to remember to make your heart beat, your lungs breathe and your stomach churn every second of every day, you would have no time for other thoughts. The brain would be overloaded with the basic processes of staying alive.

The **autonomic** nervous system could be called the *automatic* nervous system. It takes care of the basic activities inside the body that keep us alive. This leaves our minds free for other thoughts.

## What the system does

The autonomic nervous system includes parts of the **peripheral** nervous system and uses many of the same nerves. It is basically a **motor** system. It carries messages from the brain to all body parts. The body processes it controls are **involuntary.** They happen without our conscious awareness.

The autonomic nervous system keeps body processes running smoothly and body conditions constant. This is known as **homeostasis.** In these tasks, the autonomic nervous system receives help from the hormonal system (see page 27). The processes it controls include the following:

- heartbeat, especially its rate and the volume of blood pumped
- flow of blood around the body in the **blood vessels**
- muscular motions of the stomach and intestines during digestion
- breathing, especially the width of the main airways in the lungs
- removal of wastes from the blood by the kidneys and bladder
- release of products from various **glands,** such as saliva, tear fluid for the eyes, sweat on the skin, and digestive juices in the intestines
- the size of the pupil, the round opening at the front of each eye, which lets light into the eye.

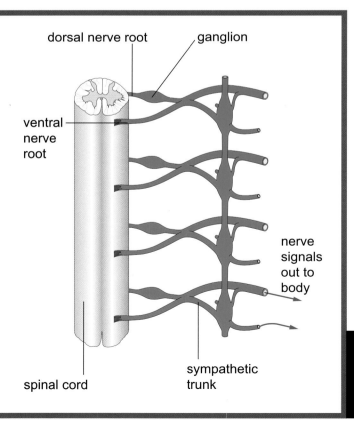

dorsal nerve root

ganglion

ventral nerve root

nerve signals out to body

spinal cord

sympathetic trunk

The autonomic nervous system includes long, nervelike parts called sympathetic trunks, which have lumps known as **ganglia** along them.

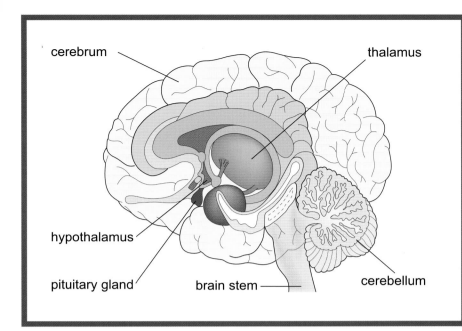

cerebrum

thalamus

hypothalamus

pituitary gland

brain stem

cerebellum

The control center of the autonomic nervous system is the hypothalamus, a small area in the middle of the lower front of the brain. Its **axons** connect to many other parts of the brain and also link directly to body parts.

## Control of the autonomic nervous system

The part of the brain called the **hypothalamus** is the body's automatic pilot. It has overall control of the autonomic nervous system. The system itself consists of two sets of nerve pathways, known as the sympathetic and parasympathetic divisions. In many cases, the two control the same body parts, but they act in opposite ways.

## Pushing and pulling

The sympathetic division is stimulatory. It makes body parts more active during times of **stress** and action, when rapid response and urgent reactions may be needed. For example, it speeds up the heartbeat, widens the eyes' pupils, and works with **hormones** to provide extra energy in the form of the sugar glucose in the blood flowing to muscles.

The parasympathetic division is inhibitory. It acts against the sympathetic division to reduce the body's processes and restore a slower, calm, resting state.

Between them, the two divisions of the autonomic nervous system control the inside of the body to suit conditions outside the body.

### The hormonal system

The hormonal, or endocrine, system is the body's second control and coordination system. It works closely with the nervous system. In general, the nervous system works over short periods of time—split seconds, seconds, and minutes. The hormonal system works over longer periods, for processes that take hours, days, and even years, such as growth and development.

# SPINAL CORD INJURY

The spinal cord is one of the best protected parts of the body. It is inside a tunnel within the backbone. In turn, the backbone is surrounded by muscles, tendons and other parts, which offer strength and stability. Despite these layers of protection, in rare cases, the spinal cord can be injured. In the United States, spinal cord injury accounts for about 1 out of every 10,000 emergency hospital visits each year.

## Main causes

Traffic accidents are the most common cause of spinal cord injury. Falls are the second most common. Sometimes, the forces involved in these events are too strong for the backbone, muscles, and other protection to withstand. The spinal cord can be severely bent, kinked, torn, or even broken if two bones in the neck or back slip across one another. The parts of the body affected depend on the site or level of the injury (see page 32).

## Falls and collisions

In a fall, the body's own weight can severely bend or crack the backbone. This may occur at one of the joints, where the vertebrae, or the disks between them, cannot cope with the **stress.** They shatter and the pieces press on, or into, the spinal cord and its nerve roots.

Other causes of spinal cord damage include sports injuries, stab wounds, gunshot wounds, and a very weak backbone, due to diseases such as bone cancer.

Rarely, players collide during sport and cause a spinal cord injury. This tends to happen when one player is moving fast and suddenly crashes into another player or players. This is especially common when the head takes the force of the crash, or when one player's neck or back becomes twisted by the weight and actions of another player. This is why suitable clothing and head and body protection are so important.

This showjumper has fallen off his horse. However, no injuries occurred because he had been taught how to fall safely.

## Whiplash

One of the most common spinal cord injuries is whiplash that occurs as the result of a traffic accident. The person's body, held by a seat belt, comes to a sudden halt with the vehicle. However, the person's head continues to move forward and jerks the neck down, banging the chin onto the chest. The head then bounces back so that the face looks upward. Even with time to tense the neck muscles, whiplash is hard to prevent. An airbag in the vehicle, and a well-adjusted headrest on the seat, can greatly reduce its effects.

Despite warnings signs such as this one, many spinal cord injuries occur each year because people are not careful and put their bodies and health at risk.

## Shallow water!

One cause of spinal cord injury, which can be prevented, is diving into water that is too shallow. The diver's head hits the bottom or an obstruction and is jerked up and back. This can smash the face and damage or even break the bones in the neck and the spinal cord inside them. The result may be loss of feeling or movement below the neck.

# FIRST AID FOR SPINE AND NERVE INJURIES

Suitable first aid for spinal cord or nerve injury can help save lives and reduce long-term damage. However, unsuitable first aid can make the damage and disability worse, and can even be fatal.

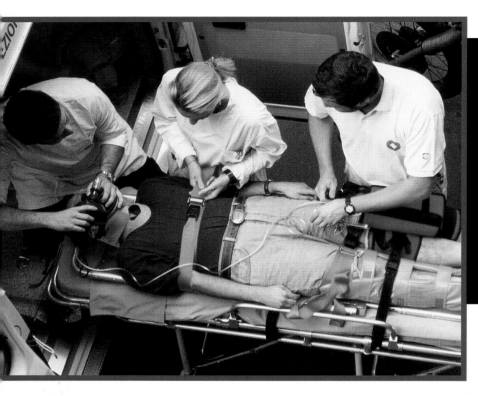

A spinal stretcher supports a patient's head, neck, and back, so that they do not move during the trip to hospital. However, putting the person onto the stretcher is, in itself, a very delicate procedure that must be done carefully to avoid nerve damage as the body parts are moved.

## Saving the spinal cord

If the spinal cord is damaged, moving a patient in the wrong way, or even at all, can increase the damage. As the patient's neck or back is bent and twisted by movement, it can squash, press, or cut the spinal cord. The same applies to other major nerves in the body and limbs.

The general advice in these situations is to leave the person in position and avoid moving him or her at all. Usually, the person is moved only if her or his life is in danger, such as from fire, poisonous fumes, machines that are out of control, or falling objects.

The key actions are
- get expert help quickly—call a doctor, paramedic, or ambulance
- make the person as warm and comfortable as possible
- support the person so that body parts cannot slip or move further
- stay calm and reassure the person.

## Conscious and unconscious

When help arrives, a conscious person may be asked questions such as, "Can you feel your feet?" and "Can you move your fingers?" The answers give clues to nerve or spinal cord damage.

An expert will check an unconscious person's heartbeat, breathing, and other signs. The expert may also check **reflex** actions and feel if various muscles are tense or floppy. The results of these tests can suggest the site of nerve or spinal cord injury.

## Transport

If there is a risk of nerve or spinal cord damage, the person is transported with great care. Supports, such as splints, are used to prevent further damage. A neck or back injury is supported by a neck collar or back brace. The person may also be strapped into a spinal stretcher, which supports the whole body.

Later, at the hospital, medical scans and **X rays** are used to check for injury. Ordinary X rays show mainly bones. Scans show nerves, **blood vessels**, and other soft parts clearly.

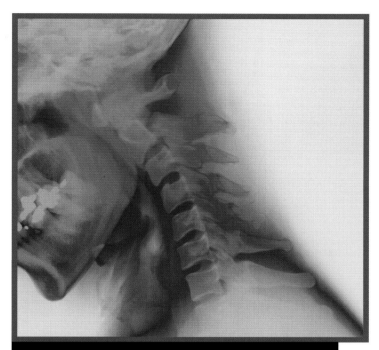

This X ray (color-coded by computer) shows a broken neck. The two uppermost vertebrae, under the base of the skull behind the jaw, are moved out of position, and the second one is fractured.

## Referred pain

Sometimes, pain is felt in one part of the body when the actual damage is some distance away. This is called referred pain. For example, the heart may suffer a temporary lack of oxygen, if a person has angina. Yet the pain seems to come from the left shoulder or left arm.

It is thought that as nerve messages for pain arrive at the spinal cord, they get mixed up with signals coming from elsewhere. The brain often thinks that the messages have come from the skin, since discomfort and pain usually happen there, rather than from parts deep inside the body.

# LEVELS OF SPINAL CORD INJURY

The effect of a spinal cord injury depends largely on the level of the injury—whether it's high up in the neck, in the chest, or lower in the back. Since the spinal cord carries **sensory** nerves traveling up to the brain and **motor** nerves traveling back down, both feeling and movement can be affected.

Sensory nerve damage leads to numbness, or lack of feeling, and perhaps aches, tingling, or pain. Motor nerve damage causes muscle weakness or **paralysis**. Either or both types of damage lead to loss of **reflexes**. The long-term outlook depends mainly on how much damage has been done.

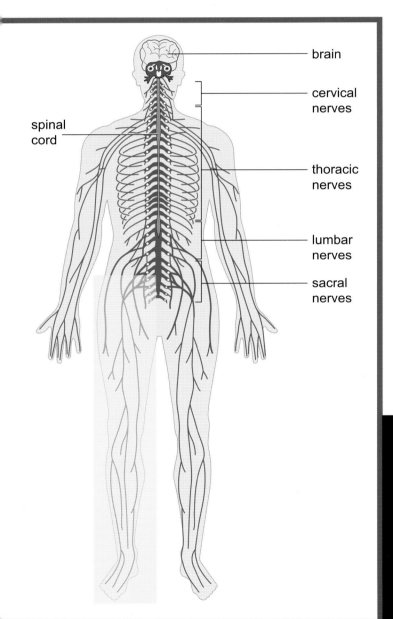

brain

cervical nerves

spinal cord

thoracic nerves

lumbar nerves

sacral nerves

## Levels of injury

In general, a spinal cord injury affects the parts of the body below its level. So if damage occurs in the lower back, numbness and paralysis tend to affect the lower body and legs. This is known as paraplegia. It may include loss of control of the bladder and bowels, lack of feeling in the skin, and the inability to walk.

If an injury occurs in the lower neck, the numbness and paralysis may affect all four limbs, which is known as quadriplegia or tetraplegia. It is sometimes referred to as paralysis from the neck down.

In an accident, the spinal cord and nerves might be injured on the right side of the sacral region. This would affect the right hip, leg, and foot, as shown. Damaged sensory nerves cause numbness, tingling, or pain, while injured motor nerves prevent movement, which is a condition known as paralysis.

An injury in the upper neck also affects the nerves that control breathing. This can be fatal. A patient injured here may recover but might need help breathing with the aid of a respirator. The real extent of a spinal cord injury may take days or weeks to become clear, because it is sometimes affected by spinal shock (see box at right).

## Long-term outlook

In some injuries, the spinal cord is swollen and bruised, but the **axons** are not broken. Usually, movements and feelings gradually return to the affected parts of the body. The injury recovers and the spinal cord heals, perhaps with the help of medication.

In other cases, surgery may be needed to try to rejoin parts of the cord's axons. The goal is to regain some feeling and movement in the future. However, this type of surgery is extremely complex and delicate, and it usually takes a long time for the patient to recover. During rehabilitation, he or she may spend many difficult weeks relearning actions that once seemed so simple, such as walking or holding a fork.

### Spinal shock
In the hours and days after a spinal cord injury, spinal shock may develop. Bruising and swelling spread along the spinal cord, so that numbness, weakness, or paralysis also spread—perhaps above the level of the injury, as well as below. In most cases, spinal shock gradually heals, but it can cause problems as doctors try to find out the real extent of the damage.

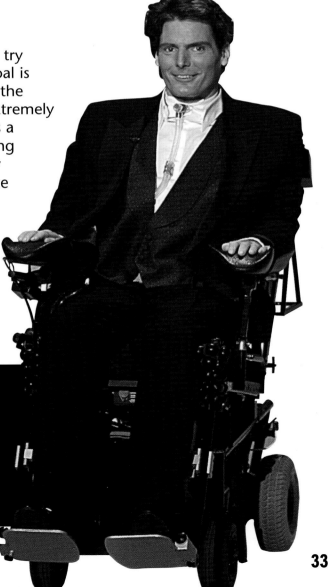

*Superman* actor Christopher Reeve has bravely battled severe spinal cord injury. He encourages others with similar conditions to stay positive and keep progressing in recovery.

# SPINAL CORD AND NERVE INFECTIONS

Germs, or harmful **microbes,** can invade the spinal cord and nerves, either by an infection of the area itself or as part of infection elsewhere in the body. **Bacteria** are germs that can generally be treated with **antibiotic** drugs. Antibiotics rarely affect **viruses,** but these germs can be treated with a growing range of antiviral medications.

## Spinal meningitis

In a healthy person, the cerebrospinal fluid around the brain and spinal cord is clear and watery. In some infections, it becomes milky or cloudy. This occurs especially in meningitis, a condition in which the **meninges,** the layers around the brain and cord, become swollen. Spinal meningitis usually results from an infection that spreads from elsewhere in the body. Rarer causes are a deep wound into the spinal cord, such as from a knife, gunshot, or severe accident.

If meningitis begins around the spinal cord, it may rapidly spread to the brain as cerebral meningitis. Symptoms include stiff neck and back, fever, nausea, vomiting, severe headache, and fear of, or pain from,

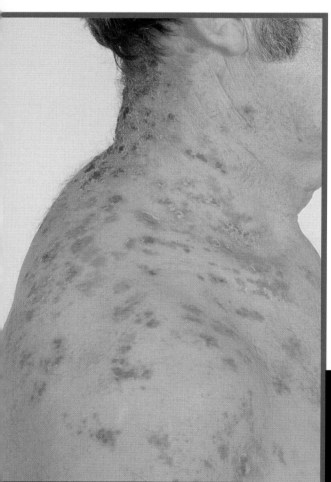

bright lights. There may also be a reddish skin rash that does not become pale if the skin is pressed. Meningitis is a serious condition and needs urgent medical treatment.

## Shingles

Shingles usually follows chicken pox, a type of virus (*varicella*) that causes itchy blisters on the skin. Some of the viruses may find their way to the nerve roots of the spinal cord and stay there, perhaps for years, causing no trouble. They may become active following another illness or emotional **stress.** Shingles causes fever; intense, sharp pains along the nerve; and an itchy red skin rash and blisters above the nerve. If shingles is discovered in time, it can be successfully treated with antiviral drugs.

Herpes viruses cause both the initial infection of chicken pox, with its itchy skin blisters, and then perhaps years later, shingles. Shingles causes skin blisters and pain from the affected nerves.

## Polio

Poliomyelitis has almost vanished from many parts of the world, due to vaccination, or shots, during childhood. However, outbreaks still occur. Polio viruses attack nerves in the lower brain and spinal cord, causing movement problems. They also cause sore throat, fever, bowel upsets, and pains and weakness in the back, arms, and legs. The affected muscles may become hard and tense or become **paralyzed**. With comfort and rest, most patients gradually recover from polio. In very rare cases, the paralysis remains.

## Secondary effects

The spinal cord and **peripheral** nerves may be affected by germs that attack other body parts. These infections include rabies, syphilis, leprosy, and diphtheria. HIV, the virus that causes AIDS, can also affect the spinal cord and nerves. It may cause a wide range of symptoms, including those described above.

In most regions of the world, the number of people with long-term disability after polio is reducing. This infection can cause life-long weakness or paralysis in a limb or body part. However, modern equipment can lessen the effects.

## Tetanus

In tetanus, *Clostridium* bacteria multiply in various body parts, such as the muscles. They produce a poison, or **toxin**, that affects the spinal cord and nerves. The muscles controlled by these nerves, usually in the limbs and back, suffer cramps and **spasms** as they become hard and painful. This may happen in the face and jaw muscles. This is why a common name for tetanus is lockjaw. If the chest and breathing muscles are involved, the infection may be fatal.

Tetanus is very rare in many areas of the world due to immunization. Treatment includes powerful drugs that make the toxins less harmful.

# SPINAL CORD AND NERVE PROBLEMS

Various medical conditions can affect the spinal cord and nerves. They range from spina bifida, which occurs during a baby's development in the womb, to the effects of aging on nerves. As people age, the skin's ability to feel and the muscles' control are less precise.

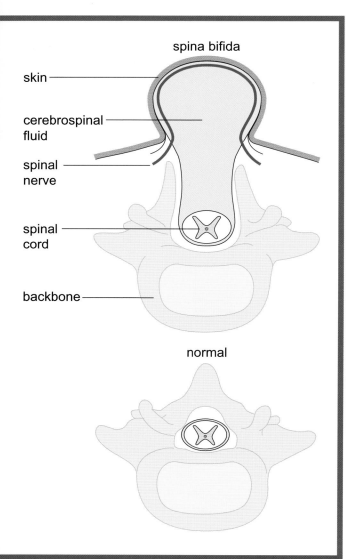

spina bifida

skin

cerebrospinal fluid

spinal nerve

spinal cord

backbone

normal

In spina bifida (top diagram) the vertebrae do not fully enclose the spinal cord as they develop in the womb. The spinal cord and **meninges** are not protected as they are normally (bottom diagram). The meninges and cerebrospinal fluid may protrude through the gap of missing bone and form a bulge under the skin.

## Spina bifida

In this **congenital** condition, the backbone does not form properly during early development in the womb. The vertebrae do not enclose the spinal cord. There is a gap along the rear of the backbone, which exposes the spinal cord. The cord itself may also be affected.

Spina bifida tends to run in families, due to a **genetic** problem. It is varied in its effects. In some cases, the affected part of the backbone is small. In others, it is more severe and there is a lack of feeling or control in the lower body, legs, bladder, and bowel. The main treatment is surgery.

## Peripheral nerve damage

Physical injury is not the only cause of nerve damage. Other causes include **peripheral** neuritis and peripheral neuropathy.

One type of nerve damage is caused by harmful chemicals called **toxins,** which somehow get into the body. They include certain pesticides; weedkillers; industrial chemicals such as lead, mercury, arsenic, and cadmium; and also various nonmedical drugs. Other cases of nerve damage are due to another condition such as an infection, **tumor,** long-term diabetes, or an **autoimmune** disorder (see page 38).

Spinal or nerve problems are no bar to staying active and taking part in exercise and sports, including at the international and Olympic levels.

## Symptoms and treatment

In most cases, peripheral nerve damage is felt as a tingling sensation that gradually spreads, for example, from the fingers up the arm. This may be followed by numbness, muscle weakness, and **paralysis.** In some cases, sharp pains shoot along the affected nerve. This is known as neuralgia.

The sooner any nerve damage is detected, the sooner treatment can begin. However, it may not be possible to heal nerve damage that has already occurred.

## Spinal tumors

Like any part of the body, tumors may occur in the spinal cord or nerves. Depending on the tumor's site and size, it can cause back pain, muscle weakness, loss of feeling, strange hot-and-cold sensations, and loss of control of the bladder and bowels. The main treatment is surgery.

### Preventable nerve damage

Some cases of nerve damage are due to a person's behavior or lifestyle. Alcohol or drug abuse or an unhealthy diet that lacks essential vitamins and **minerals** can affect the spinal cord and peripheral nerves. These conditions can have an even more serious effect on the brain. The resulting damage may cause weakness and paralysis, so the person cannot move around, and numbness, which brings the risk of further injury.

### Guillain-Barre syndrome

Guillain-Barre syndrome is a sudden, severe attack of nerve damage. It may be brought on by a viral illness or, in very rare cases, by an immunization. The person may need intensive hospital treatment, especially if breathing is affected. In most instances, the person recovers gradually.

# SPINAL CORD AND NERVE DISORDERS

Multiple sclerosis (MS) is usually a long-term condition that affects nerve **cells.** In particular, it affects the outer coverings, or **myelin** sheaths, of their **axons.** It is usually due to an **autoimmune** problem. This means that the body's **immune system,** which normally fights against germs and other invaders to protect against disease, fails to work properly. It turns against its own cells and attacks them.

## The immune system

In MS, white blood cells, known as T-cells—which are part of the immune system—act in a faulty way. They attack a substance, called

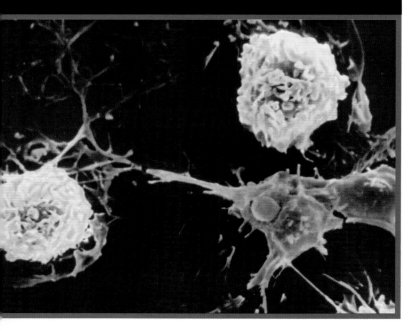

In MS, the myelin sheaths around axons are damaged. This may occur because cells called oligodendrocytes (shown here in purple), which help to form and nourish the myelin, are attacked by the body's own defense system (shown here in yellow).

myelin, which is found in the myelin sheath around each axon. This damages the myelin and the cells that make it. Nerve messages cannot pass normally along the axon.

After several attacks, the myelin and axons are stiffened, or sclerosed, by hard, scarlike material. The nerve cell may not be able to send any nerve messages.

## Effects of MS

Multiple sclerosis can affect a few or many body parts. In **sensory** nerves, it causes strange sensations, such as tingling and numbness. In **motor** nerves, it leads to loss of muscle power and coordination and perhaps loss of bladder and bowel control.

MS may disappear after one attack, or it may come back more severely each time.

MS affects about 1 person in 700 to 1,000. However, this varies greatly among different ethnic groups, and it also depends partly on where a person lives and where he or she grew up. The condition tends to begin at about the age of 20 to 30 years, and it tends to run in some families. It may be triggered by a viral infection, such as measles or herpes. There are many forms of treatment, depending on how the individual is affected.

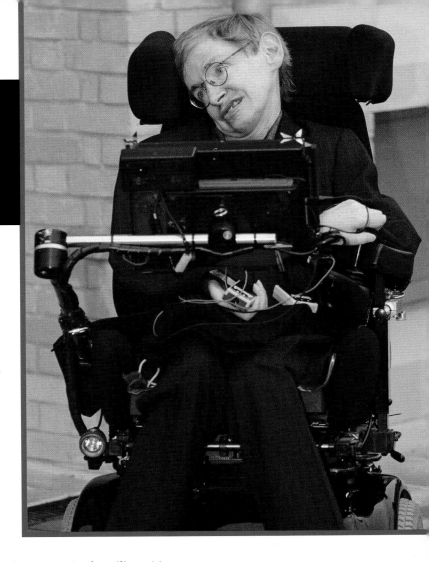

Stephen Hawking is one of the world's most famous and respected scientists, despite a nerve disorder that restricts his speech and other movements.

## Motor neuron disease

Motor neuron disease (MND) causes damage to motor nerve cells that carry messages from the brain to the muscles. There are various forms of the disease. In amyotrophic lateral sclerosis (ALS), motor nerve cells in the brain and spinal cord are affected. The muscles they control, especially in the hands and those used for breathing, speaking, chewing, and swallowing, become weak and waste away.

All types of MND are rare, and a few run in families. However, the causes are not clear. Most cases begin after the age of 50 years and take several years to progress. There is no standard, effective treatment.

### Myasthenia gravis

Myasthenia gravis (MG) affects the workings of the **neurotransmitter** acetylcholine, as mentioned on page 13. This chemical passes messages between nerve cells, especially in the **peripheral** nervous system. MG is an autoimmune disorder that attacks the places where acetylcholine has its effect, on the cell **membranes** of nerve cells and muscle cells. As a result, the affected muscles become weak and poorly controlled—from a drooping eyelid to difficulty in breathing. There are various treatments, including drugs and surgery.

# DRUGS AND THE NERVOUS SYSTEM

The nervous system is based on body chemicals. Even its tiny electrical pulses, which represent nerve messages, are made by moving chemicals. This is why more chemicals, in the form of medical drugs, can be useful to treat disorders of the nervous system. Many of these drugs affect the central nervous system—the brain and spinal cord. Fewer have their main actions on **peripheral** nerves.

## Stimulants

A **stimulant** increases activity of the nervous system, making the body more tense and ready for action. The person has greater awareness and perhaps temporary feelings of alertness and well-being. Much of this stimulant effect is because of extra activity in the sympathetic part of the **autonomic** nervous system, as described on page 27.

Mild stimulants include caffeine in tea, coffee, and cola drinks, and nicotine in tobacco. More powerful stimulants are amphetamines, benzedrine, and methedrine.

## Depressants

A depressant drug does not necessarily cause feelings of depression, sadness, and hopelessness. Instead, it depresses, or slows down, nervous system activity. Its effects are generally opposite to those of a stimulant. They include relief of tension, anxiety, and worry, which may bring on temporary feelings of well-being, as well as drowsiness and, perhaps, confusion.

Dental work would be much more uncomfortable if there were no anesthetic drugs to dull nerve sensations for pain.

Most depressants act on the brain. Alcohol, or ethyl alcohol, affects the action of acetylcholine and other **neurotransmitters**. Some **tranquilizer** drugs also do this.

Some depressants are addictive, so a person develops a need to keep taking them. In larger doses, many depressants cause harmful reactions and nervous system damage.

40

## Painkillers

Painkillers, or **analgesics,** relieve or kill pain sensations and work mainly within the central nervous system, including the spinal cord. There are two main groups: nonopiates and opiates. Many opiates are made from natural sources, such as plants. They include codeine, methadone, and morphine. These drugs help to reduce the number of pain messages that nerves send up the spinal cord to the brain.

The body produces its own opiate-like painkillers known as endorphins. These can have the same effect on the spinal cord and brain as opiates. If the body is under great **stress** or danger, yet also in pain, endorphins can help to lessen the pain, while the body deals with the stress and danger.

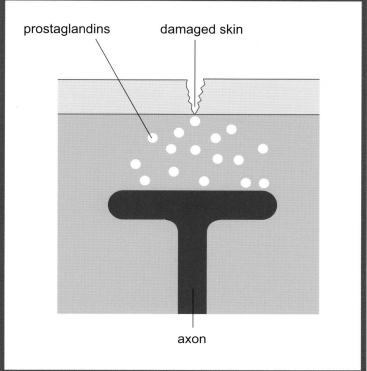

prostaglandins    damaged skin

axon

When the body is injured, by a cut in the skin for example, the damaged cells release natural chemicals called prostaglandins. These affect nerve endings and send signals to the brain, where they are experienced as pain. Some painkilling medications work by preventing prostaglandins from having this effect.

### Prostaglandins
Prostaglandins are natural body substances similar to **hormones.** Some affect the ways in which nerve processes work. There are dozens of prostaglandins. They are made in many parts of the body and cause many different effects. Some are made when a body part is damaged. They help send pain signals along peripheral nerves so that the brain is warned of the harm. The familiar painkilling drug aspirin works partly by stopping these prostaglandins.

The nervous system is very delicate and specialized. In some cases, injury cannot be repaired, nor disease healed. However, recent progress in medical drugs and surgery is leading the way to better treatments and a better outlook for millions of people.

## Neurosurgery

A single nerve **cell** with its **axon** is too small to see with the unaided eye. However, operating magnifiers or microscopes allow surgeons to see tiny bundles of nerves. Using especially small instruments, such as scalpels and forceps, surgeons can operate on nerves with amazing skill. Laser scalpels are often used, because a laser beam can be aimed very precisely to cut and heat-seal tiny areas.

This amazing technology is used to reattach body parts that have been cut off during an accident. Such operations are long and complex. Different medical teams work to rejoin nerves as well as **blood vessels,** muscles, tendons, and other parts. If the nerves are rejoined successfully, the body part may recover some feeling and movement. However, as the axons connect, they may not make the same links as they did before. This alters the nerve pathways that were familiar to the brain. The person may have to retrain both the brain and the nerves and gradually relearn movement skills.

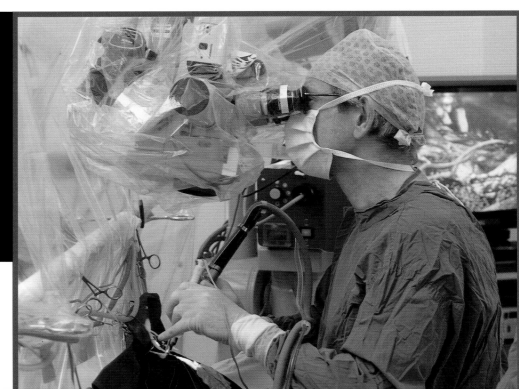

Nerve surgery is greatly helped by operating microscopes. They allow the surgeon to see and work on individual axons.

## Nerve-growing chemicals

If a **peripheral** nerve is cut or damaged, the individual nerve cells may regrow parts of themselves. This natural repair can take weeks or months, if it happens at all. It is even slower, and often less successful, in the spinal cord.

However, this nerve repair can be made faster and more successful by substances called nerve-growth, or neurotrophic, factors. Scientists have discovered some of these while researching the nervous system early in life, when it is rapidly developing. Others have been found through tests on nerve cells that have been grown outside the body, in the laboratory. The nerve-growth chemicals encourage nerve cells to send out new **dendrites** and axons and to make new connections.

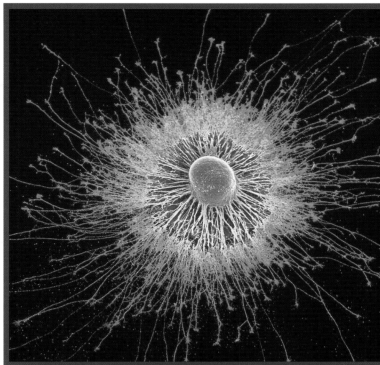

This colored electron micrograph scan shows a piece of spinal cord with the axons around it.

### New nerve cells for old

A new area of research for problems of the nervous system and other body systems is the use of stem cells. Stem cells are cells that have not yet become specialized to do a certain job. One day, scientists may be able to grow stem cells, perhaps from the umbilical cords of new babies, that will be able to specialize into nerve cells. These cells could replace nerve cells lost through injury or disease.

## The most vital system

All parts and systems of the body are important, but the spinal cord and nervous system are especially so. They carry information throughout the body and to and from the brain. Nerves control and coordinate many body processes and parts, which keep us alive and healthy. They also bring information from the senses to the brain so that you can see, hear, and feel your surroundings and smell and taste your food. Nerves also carry information away from the brain to the muscles so that you can carry out a vast array of actions and movements, from breathing, eating, and writing to running, jumping, and playing sports.

# WHAT CAN GO WRONG WITH THE SPINAL CORD AND NERVES?

This book explains the different parts of the nervous system (except the brain), how they work, and how they may be damaged by injury and illness. This page summarizes some of the problems that can affect the nerves and spinal cord, especially in young people. It also gives you information about how each problem is treated.

Many problems can be avoided by simple, practical health measures such as exercising regularly, getting plenty of rest, eating a balanced diet, and taking care when engaging in high-risk activities. This table shows some of the ways you can prevent injury and illness.

Remember, if you think something is wrong with your body, talk to a trained medical professional, such as a doctor or your school nurse. Regular medical checkups are another very important part of staying healthy.

| Condition | Cause | Symptoms | Prevention | Treatment |
|---|---|---|---|---|
| prolapsed or slipped disk | the **cartilage** disk between two vertebrae may be weak or injured, and a bulge or prolapse presses on a spinal nerve or on the cord itself | pain, numbness, and weakness at the site of the bulge in the neck or back and perhaps in the parts connected by that nerve | take measures to prevent injury to the neck or back—use protective equipment in risky sports or hazardous pursuits, wear a seat belt in vehicles, and lift and carry heavy loads correctly or ask for help | rest, pain medication, physical therapies including physical therapy, chiropractic therapy, and specific exercises; in some cases surgery may be necessary |
| spinal meningitis | infection by germs such as **bacteria** or **viruses** that spread from elsewhere or enter through a deep wound into the cord | stiff neck and back, fever, nausea, vomiting, severe headache, extreme sensitivity or pain from bright light, reddish skin rash | take general precautions to prevent neck and back injury, especially those to avoid a penetrating wound from sharp objects; wear protective and safety equipment | immediate medical treatment, which includes **antibiotics** or similar drugs and nursing care and support |

| Condition | Cause | Symptoms | Prevention | Treatment |
|---|---|---|---|---|
| carpal tunnel syndrome | pressure on the median nerve in the wrist due to injury, a disorder that affects the joints such as arthritis, repeated wrist/finger movements such as certain computer operations, or hormonal changes in the female body especially in middle age | tingling and numbness in parts of the hand, pain that is worse at night because the body is inactive and the pressure on the nerve is not relieved or shifted by movement | using suitable clothing or guards to protect the wrist from injury; avoiding repetitive wrist and hand movements; resting and stretching the hand and fingers regularly | rest, **anti-inflammatory** drugs by mouth or injection or surgery to loosen the carpal ligament. Some alternative therapies, such as acupuncture, have been found to be effective |
| spinal cord injury | neck or back damage due to a traffic accident, fall, high-speed collision, diving into shallow water, or similar physical injury | vary greatly depending on the site and severity of damage, from pain and numbness in an arm or leg to numbness and **paralysis** of the whole body below the neck | protecting the neck and back at all times, including wearing seat belts in vehicles, taking care on ladders or where falls are a risk, using protective equipment in hazardous sports or pursuits | depends on severity, but may include emergency medical care, rest, and pain medication and possibly surgery, physical therapy, specific exercises, and perhaps long-term mobility aids |
| shingles | infection by a type of virus (varicella), usually following chicken pox | fever, intense sharp pains along a nerve, and itchy red skin rash and blisters above the nerve | following general measures for good health and coping well with severe **stress** and emotional upset | antiviral drugs, rest, pain medication, and lotion or cream to reduce blistering and inflammation |

 FURTHER READING

Goldstein, Margaret J. *Everything You Need to Know about Multiple Sclerosis.* New York: Rosen, 2000.

Olesky, Walter. *The Nervous System.* New York: Rosen, 2000.

Stille, Darlene R. *The Nervous System.* Danbury, Conn.: Scholastic, 2000.

# GLOSSARY

**analgesic**  pain-reducing or pain-relieving medication

**anti-inflammatory**  reducing inflammation (swelling, redness, soreness, and, perhaps, pain)

**antibiotic**  type of medical drug that kills bacteria

**autoimmune**  when the body's immune system fails to work properly and harms its own cells and parts

**autonomic**  able to work on its own or carry out actions by itself

**axon**  long, thin part or fiber that carries nerve signals away from a nerve cell body

**bacteria**  group of microorganisms that can cause infections

**blood vessels**  network of tubes that carry blood around the body

**cartilage**  tough, strong, slightly flexible body substance, sometimes called gristle

**cell**  microscopic unit or building block of a living thing. The body is made up of billions of cells.

**cell body**  main part of a cell

**congenital**  present at birth

**dendrite**  thin, branching part of a nerve cell that carries nerve signals toward the cell body

**fibrous**  made of stringy or threadlike parts or fibers

**gamma globulin**  substance in the blood, some of which is made to fight invading germs

**ganglia**  lumplike bulges, especially along nerves

**genetic**  having to do with genes, which are the instructions for life and exist as the genetic material known as DNA

**gland**  body part that makes and releases a product (usually a liquid), such as a hormone

**hemorrhage**  leak of blood, bleeding

**homeostasis**  a state in which the conditions inside the body are constant and stable

**hormone**  natural chemical substance that affects the workings of specific body parts

**hypothalamus**  small part of the brain concerned with vital life functions. It has close links to the hormonal system

**immune system**  body's defense mechanism against infection and disease

**involuntary**  happening without the need for thought or decision; that which you cannot control

**ion** tiny particle of a substance, such as a mineral, which is positive or negative

**membrane** skinlike covering or lining layer

**meninges** three layers of membranes wrapped around the spinal cord and brain

**microbe** very small living thing, only visible under a microscope

**mineral** one of a number of chemicals needed by the body in very small amounts. Calcium and iron are minerals.

**motor** having to do with muscles and the movements they make

**myelin** fatty substance wrapped around certain axons

**neurotransmitter** chemical substance that passes a nerve message from one nerve cell to the next, across a junction or synapse

**nucleus** central part of a cell that contains the genetic material known as DNA

**paralysis** inability to move

**peripheral** around the edge, away from the middle or center

**receptor** place or site that receives or accepts a specific substance, similar to the way a lock receives a key

**reflex** body reaction that occurs quickly and automatically in response to a certain action

**sensory** having to do with detecting or sensing conditions, substances, or energy, such as the eyes, which sense light rays

**spasm** involuntary muscle contraction that occurs without warning

**stimulant** substance that stimulates or speeds up body processes, thus increasing activity

**stress** adverse, difficult, or challenging condition, which can include physical fatigue, lack of food, or emotional worry

**synapse** junction or gap between two nerve cells

**toxin** harmful or poisonous substance

**tranquilizer** substance that slows down body processes

**tumor** abnormal growth or swelling that may or may not be malignant, or cancerous

**virus** very small microorganism that can cause infection

**voluntary** happening only after you think or decide to do it; that which you can control

**X ray** form of energy, as rays or radiation, that passes through soft body parts such as flesh, but that is stopped by hard parts such as bones

# INDEX